CW0034164 6

Graft

Brian Henry

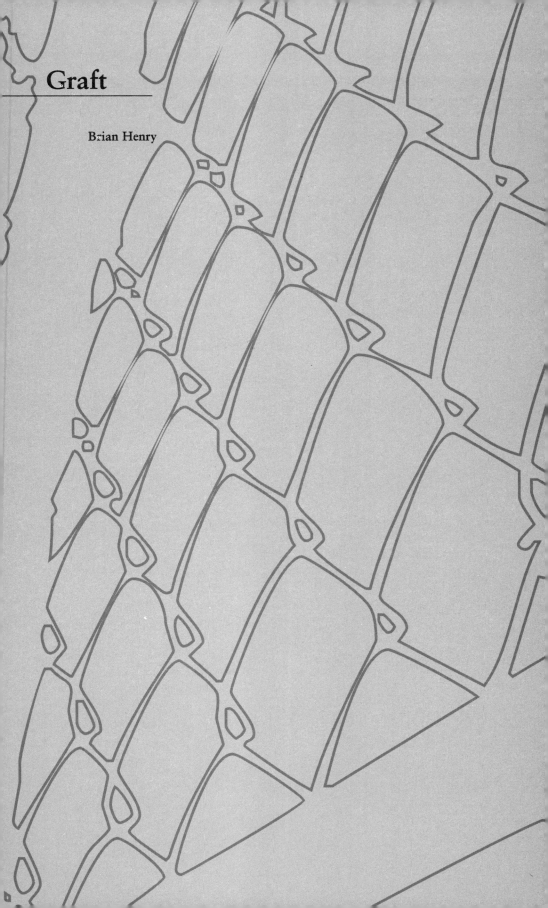

New Issues Poetry & Prose

A Green Rose Book

New Issues Poetry & Prose
The College of Arts and Sciences
Western Michigan University
Kalamazoo, Michigan 49008

First Edition, 2003.

ISBN   1-930974-32-9 (paperbound)

Library of Congress Cataloging-in-Publication Data:
Henry, Brian
Graft/Brian Henry
Library of Congress Control Number: 2003104651

Editors	Eric Hansen
	Jonathan Pugh
	Herbert Scott
Art Director	Tricia Hennessy
Designer	Allison Spicer
Production Manager	Paul Sizer
	The Design Center, Department of Art
	College of Fine Arts
	Western Michigan University

Graft

Brian Henry

New Issues

WESTERN MICHIGAN UNIVERSITY

Graft

Also by Brian Henry

Astronaut
American Incident

for Tara

Contents

I.

Reclined Nude

I saw a woman once—through her
to tell the truth—whose body
must be mine.

Her hair reflected a different light
but her eyes were green, tongue
blue, nipples pink.

Her legs rose so far above her feet
they soared.

I know those legs, the tight expanse
that moves in bounds, the dimples
beneath the ass.

I watched her so hard she forgot
it is I, not she,

who hangs at another's mercy.

Hybrid Aspects

I look forward to the impossibility of forgiveness
after knowledge, to the sweat each step entails.
The muscles associated with movement will stretch
past their zone of regular use, the bones will yank from the pressure—

this is when, if not how, objectives are met:
by the application of force within the limits of faith,
by the destruction of faith in the face of hunger.

This hunger has limits—the limits of faith—but no force.
This hunger has faith—the mind's faith in limits—but no force.
The desired will not be brought by hunger alone:

It must be met with equal parts hatred and love,
only then will it be subdued.
It must be approached with equal parts caution and bold,
only then will it be found.

Enough is to be lost by inattention. Nothing is to be gained.
The trap of particulars will close faster than that of abstractions.
But its pain, being limited to specifics, is a lesser pain.
This is what any god will tell you. This is what any god wants you to forget.

The pain in the details is a lesser pain. The pain in the lack of details,
the pain abstraction surrounds, will undo you.
This is the pain you must forget. Only then
will you find your body a shock in another's.

There can be no disappointment, no misunderstanding.
No sin of regret, or of forgetting to regret.
Only the body you desire a ruin beside yours.

And the anger of the gods whose bodies are now yours.

The hunger of those gods. Such a nothing beside yours.

Look Around

Sometimes I wonder about the power of invention.
If a look can replace the vigor I'm missing.
The woman I'm watching does not notice me.
Monday she brings petals with their stalks to her window.
Friday she removes them dried from the sill.
Her weekends are spent flowerless yet apart.
This is her summer habit and one I've come to own,
if not to love, for the habits I love are my own.
One manner of heartbreak is more abstract
than one manner of lust; this inequality
will expand to embrace what it will.
I once thought she smiled at me as I typed.
I returned the smile into the darkness
but I refuse to say *the darkness smiled back.*
The darkness was not even that dark.
The light from my computer screen at times
distracts me from my windowside vigil.
The window is a marshal of sainthood.
The window knows its job, and does it.
I have no job but to watch, and this I do
daily, and with the joy resignation brings.
Sometimes I wonder about the loss this entails.
Sometimes I wonder if my vision opens
only for windows, how I will navigate my life
in a cell. If a harbinger of spring is really desire
or only the private awareness of what
the woman I'm watching decides is her hell.
I have seen no demons in her apartment.
No demons have entered or left during my vigil.
But a demon arriving before I began
could be there still, awander in the rooms
and wanting to ask about the flowers but afraid
to ask would risk a warmth. Across the street
my apartment is cold despite the air.
Her flowers would not survive here.
But then, they will not survive anywhere.

This Blueness Not All Blue

It resembled a sun but could feather

It resembled a woman who spun
into what she touched slowly

What she touched resembled the residue of sound
that burned anyone within hearing

You walked into it and were burned

You smoldered in degrees of distraction
until the she it resembled kneeled to carry

you into a room furnished by the heat
in your head and a pain to shake your lungs dry

The sound of the touch of the she it resembled
seared into your scrap of a body as you

slipped from those arms and wondered
what it wouldn't have been like to fly

Voices Like This

I resist this beginning and hope it does not last.
I resist it because I have no place at the start.

My preference is to wash the landscape down with a stare
before stepping into what I have established.

Hence my love for rivers, for any water that's moving.
Hence my resistance to the I's presence too soon.

If I could wear what I hear, the world would own me.
As I own nothing, I try to hear what is said to me.

One could say I move in a different country.
One could say I have lost the urge to listen.

This would explain some of what requires explanation.
One could call this a virtue. One could call it a sin.

The words on the phone, because I could not catch them,
severed me from those who spoke them.

The woman in front of me, her knee
has withdrawn beneath the table as if to conceal.

If I were crouched beneath the table
the words I'd hear would match the words I would say.

The music of her legs, an exhalation I'd embrace,
would produce a note that, when repeated, I'd understand.

I support understanding. I support communication
between the mouth and the leg, the mouth and the mouth.

It should not surprise that I support communication
between the mouth and the cunt, the mouth and the cock.

If a mouth seeks congress with an ass, an ass with a cock,
I support the understanding sought. And so

with the meeting of mouth and breast, breast and cock.
The table's role in this is clearer than when I began.

If I were seated there she would know I have no secrets.
The secrets I have interest only me.

If she asked me to tell her something interesting
I'd feel the pull of narrative, the nostalgia it brings.

I would be forced to admit I know nothing of interest.
I prefer this to inventing a tale for the purpose.

Her knee has not emerged from the table
where, I've noticed, she sits alone.

Of course she is enveloped in blue, her hair brown as it descends.
It descends past her shoulders, the collarbone I can see.

Because I have no language I must repeat what I hear.
She says nothing, I have no words to repeat.

If she moves her knee into view I will approach.
If she moves her mouth as if to speak I will repeat the motion.

The silence the phone has brought between us
has not brought us closer.

It is no strange thing to have the look of prayer
when a body is the main concern.

Because her body is the main concern
there can be no part of her I will not revere.

My mouth, when it moves, will move for her.
This posture I offer to bring me closer.

I am no closer than when I began.
Because her tongue, like her knee, remains unseen

I maintain the posture. I must step to her and motion
as if my mouth to move. I must step to her

and motion as if my mouth to move.

This Blueness Not All Blue

That is the point where we undid each other.
Unzipped each other, shook each other
onto the snow. The point where we rescued each other
from the cold, bundled each other into packets to cradle.
Where you promised no more pleading *tomorrow,*
tomorrow as you'd done since I'd met you
at the station, under the awning, before the last train arrived.
That is the point I lifted your blue cable sweater
from your body and covered with my hands all I could cover
and tasted all my hands could not hold.
The point where you asked me inside, as I was,
perpendicular beneath the skylight that offered a view
of more dead suns than anyone could count.
As the number of times you asked me inside you that night,
that week, are more than anyone could count.

Graft

The woman pinching her nipples
with increasing force
does not practice for her lover's bite
whatever her lover whispers
to himself in bed with himself.

The woman pinching her nipples
with the other hand below
thinks, perhaps, of the crocus
pushing through the dead
matter of the yard, *as if in offering*
or insistence of its virtues
hidden until its moment
arrives, pushing, with it.

This, at least, is what her lover thinks
she thinks; what he fears
she thinks is another matter:
another man, a woman like her
in build and demeanor,
a stranger seen for five seconds
then, now, obliterated by her hands.

This Blueness Not All Blue

For to remember her is to invite movement
where stasis, at last, was achieved.

The areolae flanking, the fabric
between mouth and mound.

The muscles of her stomach,
the way they curved inward and down.

One leg poised on my shoulder,
the other behind, on the bed.

There was no song there,
the music no music to remember.

How I inhaled the air around,
as close to breathing itself

as a mouth could bring.

A Distant Architecture

1st

The day's languid tongue pulls the moisture
of our bodies to the surface.
You'd better fuck me before the hot.
The sun, stricken for days, pulses
bleary with its own pollination:
yellow dust ransacks the atmosphere,
the car, the pond, the tar of the road
coated in a daze of asphyxiation.
We converge on the narrow bed:
your legs will not spread wide enough
to allow for the loosening
to let you come
so you lean back, arc
from me with me still inside,
rub yourself to an edge

2nd

Everywhere you go there's weather.
Everywhere you go something begs you
to resist it.
This passion for withered things dooms you
to particulars.
Even pastimes have passed you,
swaying into the water-
logged cushions, awash in the musty residue.
Whatever you hold onto, less remains:
you lift skin
from surface to surface and skin remains
to be lifted.
Somehow you will climb into the creases of her hand
and make your home there.
Somehow you will grasp what it means
to merge one life with another.
The air, so dry
it could ignite with the thought of fire,
wavers visibly

3rd

That which has taken hold cannot be held
through the festive gloss
applied (by the people) (to the heat).
A margin of error, a wide
margin of error, can be found
wherever waterlines are broken,
the swell of fluid's lack
throbs in the ground,
knocks through the walls he and she refuse to own
but must call their own as long as
they have no place to call

This Blueness Not All Blue

absents itself from its vapors
before the pilaster,
a cautionary instance of color.

Vacancy matters less than volition
when joining one to another,
my ribs riding your mutinous face to snow.

No part of her not shedding in my mouth,
no part not held in the attempt to lift
the soul from the body containing it.

In the Midst of the Harshest Winter
We Continue Touching With Our Burns

How can I map your body with tenderness,
take away no more than is needed,
when mapping requires a constant
violence against specifics
as desire takes over the mind of the task?

Like when I look at you through the bottom
of my glass: the you I see matches the you
I know, but is twisted, an atom
or two has slid out of alignment and dropped
its true self to carry another self
no less you for having shifted
the weight of what, at first, seems burden.

The surface of what is mapped, so delicate
yet full of lust despite the surface,
withstands whatever is brought upon it
unless the wind clears what already is flat,
divests the terrain of details and tells
the stylus which way to forge along the page,
now thoroughly smudged with mistakes.

As if the creation of a map replaced discovery.
As if the map were its own invasion
into territory always known but not named
into submission. This cartographer's sin,
if he sins, is loving what he ruins.

Gesture

Having lost her in her sleep
beside you, you twist the thought
of the day she spent without you

as if the motion could draw light
to what you know
you cannot see, never will.

Something in her breath less rasp than heave
pulls you out of the self
bearing down on your sleep:

you try to will her to touch
and when she does
—an ankle across your shin—

the shock of what's inside you
grows into its own pain,
that which gives until the fear of giving

is gone.

River Versions

When I say her look lacerated me
I am using hyperbole to describe
how the emotional felt physical to me

         the physical her house to dwell in

    a lurch behind the eyes

        distinguishable flush in a world of

2.

Tired of chronology I broke
         her fear snapped
cold and wet in my hand

Four layers of ice between us
         and the ground
Not the mud at the bottom
         but the mud beneath
The third layer pocks the ice
         though only near the river

3.

Rain will fall tonight into snow
the river swell and freeze

and freeze to add a fifth layer
to this insistent wetness

4.

More than the fear of dying
brings two people to pieces
together

The cost of giving and the cost of being
brought to a place as a pair

The end of something
not (she said)
the start of something

False Winter

The suffering that wrings through our mouths
pushed below the waterline
by weight not our own, and by our own,
we mix along the fissures asleep,
drunk like young fathers.

The mountains admit no attempt at prayer,
they offer no abstract song.
Real snow falls only once:
all other winters are an imitation.

A fucked reckoning is in store for those
—us—who obsess over what they've lost
instead of what they've been offered: a point
where forgetting is its own preposition,
the link between *and* and *between*, the of

of all we've learned but have managed
to bring through our years and call new life—

Flood

Whoever said passion is overrated, spent in these yellowed
ruins when compared to the antics of the oil tank and the fuel line,

neglects the decline in values bemoaned in this nothing of a town
and beyond, at the submerged bridge, the bubbling river draining,

at the diner, full of smoke, forgiving in girth if not flow:
by no means will anything collapse today, least of all the tower

with the bronze bust on its spire, or the concert hall,
deliciously derelict these past two hours yet whole.

Between the riverbank—where it was—and the floodline,
a child, dim in mind and fortune, lies tangled and thick, brittle

in the crannies of swell and recede, the ice this year especially volatile,
they say, a thing to watch, beware of.

Across the river

a bull moose waits
(for something)
to cross the river. Finally it crosses.
You want to link the moose
to the pain in your chest
but to compare
a moose's efforts to ascend a riverbank
at dusk, in the heat,
to your own life—

So you watch it go, and let the impulse go
with it, over and out
of view of the zero stars
governing a sky
increasingly savage in its clearness.

Fetched in the Storm

In lieu of retraction or retreat, she pushes
further into the interior addled by dusk.

The wet means little cracks beneath,
means a bare line of vision before.

His distance grows, she hopes, with speed,
to a less.

This is how a story comes around—
to scores already tallied, moments

forgotten hastily, as quick or quicker
than they'd happened. *Whose story?*

not a thing to ask but to think about.
Penetrating, she moves discernibly

through the covering, metal's gleam
in front of her, the sound of cutting absent.

In front of her, just past where she can see,
a man cannot but trip over the roots

he thinks are reaching for him, his body
gathering abrasions rapidly but with small pain.

Each trip slows him, she does not trip
and therefore gains, she does not trip

and sees him sliding down a bank,
runs because she knows the river there

—its depths no depths at all—
because she prefers shooting down, coming down upon.

He clutches at roots as he slides,
at sticks, and stops at the river's edge

to think a way across:
he chooses to wade and swim

as quick across as his body allows,
will dive if she comes upon him shooting.

She comes upon him singing.

Between the River's Curves

Having forgotten to follow him across the river, I trail (the edge)
for miles as if miles could shrink distance down, tighten the gap between.

The river's curves and the bank's decline, the darkness, the silted ground,
I lose ground on the man I am, until now, pursuing (out of need).

The fragrance of fragments diminishes the lines I have drawn—windy map—
by turns I lose my head and footing, my clean line (silt-smeared).

Pursuit in this place is a way of life, as is loss (of what one pursues),
but what sucks is the time spent en route to what, at last, is no at last.

What sucks is this intrusion into what started as action (at least motion),
this failure to close with a gesture that manages more than failure (to close).

A Fortune Lost in Terror

In two's behind the shed by the river
Enough remains to be said   & done
To keep all the boys real busy
Not a chance of sinking sunk
Sunk before the proper time
He belts himself his words instead
& shouts to trees to heat theirselves
For this position is more than stance
When the sun has pulled away from what
Pokes & scrapes his legs where he's crouched
& waits for a branch to shake him in half
& waits for the water to wake & shove
The leaves from where they dared to rest

II.

Winter, With Demons

This outward profusion of bruises surfaces in untidy phalanges.
They stumble upon that which has stumbled: a color cut and followed.
One screams river when so swollen, it screams river
though no water crosses; and lake, lake assumes some feeder.
This quagmire a scattering loose and stark: one screams swamp,
swamp in which skin's tripwire churns to pieces
its pilots who have no who about them and persist
in blankness, that blackness tinged with blue, blue-colored blue.

The palette repels more than it absorbs.
Taut square whose curves unite angles
of ill design under the tongue's slow bulge:
rib, breast, collarbone; the small of the back;
the stresses and dips; the cracks; the pores—
these too repel more than they absorb.
The palette is scoured anew and cast
onto glaciered shores.

A tongue cracked and sore from listening to the folds
: a splinter a thorn a shard that slips against this shore
: a slide a hill a cure that knows no curve
: an arch a knot for the flab of the neck a neck
: a pillar a pylon a fountain that shimmers when approached
: a bridge a darkness a series of surfaces intact
: a crash a clamor an instant without wires
: a dampness between the eyes a darkness a dampness

The End of Winter

or not a place you choose to visit
south of a hurt from years before
when you were lost among ice and trees
and slept in the muddied slush

when you followed a girl further
than intended and were turned away
beaten out of her house by her father
flushed with something akin to rage

when your tongue leapt to find a path
into your friend's mouth, down his pants
and along the base of him, and beyond
and his brother ground your face into the rug

or when you broke a man's shin
with a board, and broke the board
and forced a jagged half down his throat
to pound until the wood blushed

and his face fell to pieces at your feet
a blossom heralding a season's demise
an ache that begins with the bones
and ends with the end of winter

Another Cross

The lake shimmers// as lakes tend
Somewhere a stone with a boy on it
Finds itself photographed// the boy too
Some kind of malice in the air
Above the houses behind the boy
Above the boy's house// and within
The lake immune to such constructions
A sliver of a stream puckering into the lake
Who said thirst who said wait
The heaviness of whatever sits
Who woke swollen the flesh
No longer palette but globe
Who laughed when the water broke

Limelight

A calcified recalcitrant,
I retract all words
the bones left behind.

Jesus Trap

Partition me and take these rivulets too.
Flap flap goes the foreskin. Snick snick.
Oh I'm a bloody mess. Reach me from behind.
I forgot where I was going when I noticed.
My vision is worse than before. My eyes.
They're fucked. I stumble so much now.
Walk into door jambs, counters, corners.
Objects my adversaries. I hit whatever.
I hit. The ground, the water. The water.
I walked across. I was walking across water.
My feet foamed. The water moved. Wet.
All across. To displace the wet without.
Sinking. To call myself Savior. Martyr.
On the carpet. The flood lifted me up.

Break It On Down

In due course one admits the sex was magnificent
Borrowed from fandangos of chance
Markers soak through your sweatered chest
Frost heaves burst from the back yard's muddle
To meet and discuss the status of hands
You wept when you gleaned what he meant
My sentiments exactly heading west
Though not often enmeshed in such a meddle
The formal entourage retiring too early
Beyond the borders of suburban power outages
That cluster of hawks swoops toward the deer
For carcasses are all that we all that we
Bless the conceptual artist for his brazen images
Know there is no knowing here

Subculture

Less about necessity than splintering of need,

you wrap yourself back into *a kiss*
might have closed it and pass off lust as leisure
discards all decoration in this city of steam.

Grim prospect, the decision to walk into the day
after waking.
                    He sweeps wax from the nightstand
into your palm, kicks out of bed with his limp.

The local voyeurs at the window, their faces masked
by moisture that freezes too fast: ardent mirror,
a flurry of abrasion delivered at last.

His flesh returns to its station in extremis, a flourish
of bad architecture better lost.
                              Steel tracks reverberate
into the mist, dogs drone from boxes and crates,
and planes descend like too many shawls in a nest of when.

At the door he turns to ask who will play nurse
to a most common demeanor (the denominator
diminished long before the fraction became improper)

and who will be left scraping a severed knuckle,
holding the notes for another to hold onto.
The blood on his neck smeared where you licked it:

the knife's dull end scorned for a sharper edge,
the eye claims for itself one last view
before all intentions are scuttled by pillars of wind.

Urge and Resist

I knelt to receive what, receiving, I feared,
washed by the light his skin created.
Nor did I pause to ask, though I paused unhindered,

if his sleep were open to one less mired
than the rest. The question, I know, was weighted
so I knelt to receive what, receiving, I feared.

Once burrowed, I tried to dwell in his marred
embrace, to remain inside him, elated.
Nor did I pause to ask, though I paused unhindered,

where his hands were going, what they fingered
—a body brushed by hands he hated?—
as I knelt to receive what, receiving, I feared.

He said nothing, yawned, answered
by removing me from him, deflated.
Nor did I pause to ask, though I paused unhindered

and left the room diminished by his disregard.
I could not see, the light outside had faded,
nor did I pause to ask, though I paused unhindered,
why I knelt to receive what, receiving, I feared.

Reclined Nude

How can I blame myself for the vision
I did my best to withstand, a blend
of assertiveness and bland persistence
that, when applied, bled into insignificance?

Well of course I blame myself, for that
and for this, an incursion of little point
or even resistance, and the tears you see
are not the tears I pretend to own. Oh dear.

I left a propeller behind at the fair; some runt
of a boy is fingering it now, its plastic edge.
I'd love to shove that edge right up his

Residue

The way the sun works the powerlines
      one could be excused for thinking
one mattered to the hill disrupting the horizon:

      footprints and tire tracks break right
at the base of, lose themselves into the woods
      rimmed with shit, the residue
of marijuana smoke clinging.

Birdsong might be strangling, but the hum
      is what we hear as the air warms below,
between, the air about to split from the attention.

This swathe affords a stellar view, the tracks
      wind endlessly. One could push a Snowcat
to its last gallon without reaching anything
      like an end; one could string a year's
worth of garbage along this scratch of land.

Walt, who jogged this route for ten years, says
      the thrum in the air will stunt growth,
says his neighbor's kids are shorter than each
      of their parents, says he himself has shrunk.

A bull and heifer escaped from the patch
      across the river once, stayed a week
before being found. All's they did was fuck

under the transformers, that cock matched
      by a cunt open—for what, pleasure?—
and the boy who found them locked, smoking,
      one wonders where he's ended up,
or if.

Reclined Nude

Lofty ideals are fine for former corporate
whores, their every missive complete
with self-promoting fliers and brochures.

I prefer the grittier way of conducting
business, refuse to blush or otherwise kneel
to whomever thinks he owns a piece of this.

I suppose it all began when my eyes gave out,
so quickly and with great pain—much much pain—
a scar in a hillside that bungles sight.

Fucking hillside, floating through the ether
as if the sky mattered, as if the trees leaning
against each other did so out of anything but spite.

Friction

Prefers his boys asleep in leather

A vein between the eyes

The last round of lovers left him raw

To weep for every pretense toward

All the friction of a space so small

The last round a vein between

Dawn when it hits splits the sonnet in two

Infirm

said of the something parted by telepathic particulars
none deserved fortune's bath
the cleavage of the matter in clear view
wants accumulated like passages
night its own coat hanger
beaten until broken the nose realigned itself with its old self
the balaclava fell with their weapons and instruments
the nullification of cement's special powers hove bone upon teeth shattering
upper ridge grating the curb the boot descends upon the skull
the powder curb-color were it not for the blood
two girls in the courtyard below count to cross purposes
there were two sounds   the sound of a body breaking
                                                the sound of numbers on the move
to hear the sound of a body breaking to blur

Here, in the Little-Ease

The clang of the martin around my neck
checkered the affair.
So many succulents passed
on suggestions for group activities,
so many roses escorted the succulents
to fêtes extraordinaires
while it grew stuffier
and stuffier in here, in the little-ease.

This issue of contest and contesting the self
extends to the body and the body's canvas,
a wealth of hues and circles to discover
and use. But the introduction
of the discussion of various viruses
tends to dampen passions otherwise
passionate, and the faces of women
and men otherwise willing
mutate as they extricate
each other from the thorniest of situations.
May they too awaken
bird-necked and desperate for action.

May they miss these insinuations.

Cosmology

A sprinkle here, a sprinkle there,
my juices have never been so free.
Fallacy of representation, remove
me from your grasp, I'm too slippery.
By nighttime I'm something else,
a pile of what's been shed and swept
by blemished feet against the wall.
Blend of dog hair, crumbs, and straw.
The interim is what I move for.
The interim is where I'm stuck
by she who won't stick me.
A stalk bursting from my loins
she tries to break a hip against.
I know my mind writhes along
the tawdriest channels, gets nasty
sometimes. At times I hoist
at an angle likely to discomfit,
wring the flesh like a soggy towel.
More often I proceed through the day
flaccid and content until a glimpse
reels me. Then I'm backonboard,
in the straddle, for the haul.
I've been told this is a bad way to be
but my nerves have a way of holding on.
My limbs lose a little smoothness every year.
My draperies flourish regardless, they flutter
about for all to see. I clung to the sill
to pry away the screen—this is how
I gained entry.

What Kind

When one sins, daily, by eating too much, drinking too much,
and fucking as much as possible, the spires are reminders:

You are always sinking, climbing lower in the valleys despite.
The flesh you consume will be what, in the end, burns first, and most slowly.

The house with no windows, one wall in pieces inside, will, if you approach
from the east, pitch glass at you, knowing you'll call it gravity.

A bird—you're not sure what kind—intersects your line of sight
to divide the space almost in half, its wings the hypotenuse

to the triangle your presence has established in this dying yard,
a presence as welcome as the sun is white, where every hill

has its village, every village a church, and the spires, modest
as they are, still manage after all these years to point upward.

Reclined Nude

I often feel the need to scratch, so scratch I do.
You wouldn't know the agony this can bring,
the hoopla it pulls a body through.

You try lying here all day, hearing what I've heard.
The worst is knowing others know I'm bored
yet do nothing, pass by undisturbed.

To be ignored when display is the aim:
an insult too great to bear.
How else can I reach out of the frame,
cause an ear to burn, or at least to ring?

Pluto's Lament

The elephantine aspect of the other planets—
I'd dredge that if I could,
so far from everything and so cold.
I'd dredge the sun for solids,
break bread with a wayward moon,
say "at any moment we can be carried
skyward, there's so little to us"
but wouldn't mean it. The truth is,
"Love at last has left her soiled drawers
on the floor." I pray to sling a bit of dust
in the faces of the men,
to rap their knuckles real sound.
Watching hardcore in the lounge,
they're out in a circle, their hands
in movement of music seen once in a face.
I could see her fillings in the money shot.

Interregnum

Upon our return an emulsified push into fourth
greeted us, our bedraggled bodies dragged
further into the depths of lotion and foam
than any skin about to burst can stand:
someone on board has earned a reprimand,
and I'll see to its delivery, to be certain.

The gall to speak of what one has seen
when winging past the moon, a week of no sleep,
as if the nine planets could align themselves
into anything but a string of mishaps . . .

Willing to sacrifice myself for something
untowardly grand, I'd been told the sun is a star,
a ball of lava bound to singe the earth
to bits in two billion years. I'd believe that
if not for all the humidity posed against
the pour, the day-long boredom of the pour.

The Power of in the Age of

I said well why not when confronted
with the sternness of a life ill-suited
to anything but conflict and conflation,

a derelict hole revolving mindlessly
before the matters of fact dictate terms
to those of us ill-used by truth and what-

not, garters and thongs awaver past dawn,
the mania for bargains breaking every
last one of the hungers (I mean hunters)

until the wax owns the car rents the road,
until the interest rates so highly the bank
manager offers to drive your small ones

to school and back as long as the principal
is up and running, though debt can grow
into its own form of tribute to plains and rivers,

the mountains between, beaches welling
at the edges—how they flank a billion passions
for cooking oneself under melanomic suns—

the remains of what you own being fucked
by what you owe, the dog spayed beyond
good breeding, and the darkest hours swelling

with intent to instill on a surface where
understanding cannot spawn but so often each day
and only then just so often,

as the boredom factor dishes out
more nothing than any sane person can take
while another branch of worries is brought

to whomever is least able to cope
with being sucked off in front of his boss
or by his boss (taking that request for a raise

Graft

Henry

too far past the point of the request):
this business of ass and balls can wear down
a man seeking sleep and dreamlessness

though the moon cutting through
the screen, the blinds must touch him here,
on his back, and here, on his arm, the one

that has worked its way from under
the sheet covering the bother he calls a body
and inching toward the end

of what everyone would call the bed,
lovely, the timing in my life is lovely
a line that stiffens through him

as he staggers downward into the sleep
he knows he needs but cannot,
desire for a moment desire's absence, a push

beneath the thoughts uncertain of the effect
they seek, but certain the effect, once achieved,
will attract whatever is needed from within.

Leverage

the crush without
matter of course
forgeries passed off
behind closed shores
the stars descend
snow into sleet
symphonic opera slut
becoming too hoarse
in case lust
its cost wanes
is it possible
to ignore surface
here for once
is it possible
to fuck alone
sleep without whores

The Company Not Kept

. . . the time to pull out the ratchet set and set
    to work like a carnival cruiser hobbled
in its harbor of sullied faces, a distracting series
    of places on parade, the light going latch
by sodden match, until the air returns
    to its darker state and the man awakes
or, more accurately, remembers his hands
    and what they're doing to that between,
and starts to whistle, less to himself than to the one
    swelling beneath him, still under the shudder
that returns him to his hands, the whistle now
    more a hiss   suspiration   rasp under the light's
own throbbing   absence, the skin honed
    like a spun thing, a single freckle perfect

in its refusal   to graph the ellipse
to broach the circle   as unequation
or replace place   before it absconds
with namesake   with the solution

the blemish focuses   his attention
or he aligns sight   wayward but wary
sets one object   of his attention
against the other   this is the final way

until clear   he thinks
the skin beneath   his hand
the skin peels   away
from the friction   he ignores the pain

of skin against skin   and the friction
of suffering   is not suffering

Notes

"This Blueness Not All Blue" is a phrase borrowed from Charles Tomlinson's "The Metamorphosis."

"Everywhere you go there's weather" (in "A Distant Architecture 2nd") is August Kleinzahler's phrase, from an interview.

"In the Midst of the Harshest Winter We Continue Touching With Our Burns" owes its title to Ales Steger.

"Fetched in the Storm" owes its title to Gerard Manley Hopkins.

The italicized phrase from "Subculture" is from Thomas Hardy's "She Charged Me."

"Pluto's Lament" uses phrases from Robert Duncan's "Yes, As a Look Springs to Its Face" and Dean Young's "Threshold."

Acknowledgments

The author is grateful to the editors of the following magazines, in which some of these poems first appeared: *The Antioch Review, Boston Review, Colorado Review, Columbia: A Journal of Art and Literature, Cream City Review, Denver Quarterly, Fence, Fulcrum, Grand Street, Interim, Island* (Australia), *The Kenyon Review, Leviathan Quarterly* (Germany), *LIT, Luna, Meanjin* (Australia), *Metre* (Ireland), *Natural Bridge, Nerve, The New Republic, Notre Dame Review, NowCulture, The Paris Review, Poetry Daily, Poetry Review* (UK), *Salt* (Australia), *Slope, Sonora Review, Third Coast, TriQuarterly, Upstairs at Duroc* (France). "This Blueness Not All Blue (2)" was reprinted in *Pleased to See Me: 69 Very Sexy Poems* (Bloodaxe Books), edited by Neil Astley. Special thanks to Donald Revell for selecting "False Winter," "A Fortune Lost in Terror," "Interregnum" and "The Power of in the Age of" for the 2001 George Bogin Memorial Award from the Poetry Society of America.

The author also would like to thank Herb Scott, David Dodd Lee, and Derek Pollard for their support; Timothy Donnelly, Henry Hart, Timothy Liu, Peter Richards, Tessa Rumsey, Tomaz Salamun, Reginald Shepherd, and Matthew Zapruder for their assistance (tangible and intangible); Andrew Zawacki for being the first reader for all of these poems and for helping the manuscript reach its final form; and Tara Rebele for sustenance in the freeze and vitality in the heat.

Brian Henry's first book of poetry, *Astronaut,* was published in the United States by Carnegie Mellon University Press, in England by Arc Publications, and in Slovenia by Mondena Publishing, and was shortlisted for the 2000 Forward Prize. His second book, *American Incident,* appeared from Salt Publishing in 2002. An editor of *Verse* since 1995, he has reviewed poetry for numerous publications, including the *New York Times Book Review, Boston Review, The Yale Review,* and *The Kenyon Review.* He teaches at the University of Georgia, where he directs the Creative Writing Program.

New Issues Poetry & Prose

Editor, Herbert Scott

C. Mikal Oness, *Water Becomes Bone*
Elizabeth Powell, *The Republic of Self*
Margaret Rabb, *Granite Dives*
Rebecca Reynolds, *Daughter of the Hangnail; The Bovine Two-Step*
Martha Rhodes, *Perfect Disappearance*
Beth Roberts, *Brief Moral History in Blue*
John Rybicki, *Traveling at High Speeds* (enlarged second edition)
Mary Ann Samyn, *Inside the Yellow Dress*
Ever Saskya, *The Porch is a Journey Different From the House*
Mark Scott, *Tactile Values*
Martha Serpas, *Côte Blanche*
Diane Seuss-Brakeman, *It Blows You Hollow*
Elaine Sexton, *Sleuth*
Marc Sheehan, *Greatest Hits*
Sarah Jane Smith, *No Thanks—and Other Stories* (fiction)
Phillip Sterling, *Mutual Shores*
Angela Sorby, *Distance Learning*
Russell Thorburn, *Approximate Desire*
Rodney Torreson, *A Breathable Light*
Robert VanderMolen, *Breath*
Martin Walls, *Small Human Detail in Care of National Trust*
Patricia Jabbeh Wesley, *Before the Palm Could Bloom: Poems of Africa*